ABOUT THE AUTHOR

CW01558470

David Mason, born 1 ... ter
University before emba... n a
large pharmaceutical c ... in
Alfresco Eating Hou... elf
employment created the ... est
in writing.

The success of his previous book persuaded him to begin performing live locally and nationally, both accompanied and solo. If you would like David to perform at a venue near you, please contact him at Alfresco Eating House (address below).

By the same author:
"Inside Out"   - More poetry by David J. Mason
"Speaking Out" - Audio collection of selected work from
"Inside Out" and "Get a life".

"Get a life" first published in 1997 in Great Britain by
David J. Mason
Publishing address:
Alfresco Eating House, Norwich Road, Ludham, Norfolk NR29 5QA.

British Library Cataloguing-in-Publication Data
A Catalogue record for this book is available from the British Library.
© David J. Mason
ISBN 0 9521326 3 X

Front cover illustration and chapter illustrations ©Nick Walmsley.
Contact address: Alfresco Eating House, Ludham, Norfolk.

This book is dedicated to Helen.
Thanks for all your support and encouragement and the hard work in bringing this book to publication.

Love, Dave

TABLE OF CONTENTS

FOREWORD   1

GET A LIFE

Get a life	4
Enlightenment	5
Ode to Geoffrey Boycott	6
Buy now, pay later	7
A struggle	8
The revolution begins	9
Suicide	10
Waste	11
In the end	12
Gutter	13
In summary	14
University Challenge	15
Worth it	16

OUR MAN IN MAJORCA

My bunion	20
Death Valley	21
A lesson	22
Pools	23
Big red boots	24
The red flag	25
Red wine	26
Just like Wordsworth	27

ALL THINGS BRIGHT AND BEAUTIFUL

The tree that holds up the sky	30
December skyline	31
Winter's words	32
Orange	33
After the rain	34
New Year's Day	35
The conservatory	36
Consider the lilies of the field	37
And a cold wind blows	38
Phew!	39
The buddleia	40

ALL CREATURES GREAT AND SMALL

Three hares	44
Skylark	45
Dog in a Fourtrak	46
The locust with one leg	47
The walkers	48
Segregation	49
In the bay	50
Observation upon, and advice to, one of life's survivors	51
A real buzz	52
Old egghead	53
The enemy within	54

DECORUM

Trying it on   58
Fashion   59
A good party   60
Holiday hopes   61
Middle-aged women are the rudest   62
Either way, it stinks   63
Out damn spot   64
The gifted child   65
Scene from a posh party   66
Stop, look and listen   67
The concerns of a frontbencher   68
Humility   69
Appearances can be deceptive   70
Real men take speed   71

ANOTHER DAY AT THE OFFICE

A corporate kiss   74
Power dressing   75
Mission statement   76
You won't want to talk to me   77
Company man   78
The questionnaire   79

PLAYING FTSE UNDER THE TABLE

Fill in the gaps	82
Paper riches	83
How to bake an immoral cake	84
Weapons of war	85
Municipal sports centres they failed to build	86
The working man and woman of no fixed class	87

IN THE PSYCHIATRIST'S CHAIR

A den	90
A break in	91
The knowledge	92
Put the past behind you	93
Who goes there?	94
William won't tell	95

WHO NEEDS DRUGS?

Atmosphere	98
The message	99
The day the world ended	100
Fire at the lido	101
The banana-yellow Allegro	102
Adrenalin	103

A NEW DAWN

Carry on	106
A clean sweep	107
Daylight	108
Exposure	109
The first coffee	110
Flashback	111
On closer inspection	112

A LITTLE GREEN PIECE

The elevated section of the M4	116
We need a bypass now! (Part 1)	117
We need a bypass now (Part 2)	118
Kids without legs	119
No holes left (in the belt)	120
Recession is a good thing	121
Injuns' revenge	122

THINKING OF YOU

The preacher	126
Old blue eyes	127
The first beat of love	128
For you, my love	129
The girl with the cigarette	130
Lenza penny	131
Love machine	132
One too many	133
Softy	134
Someone's mother	135
Stranger	136
A wasted journey	137

FOREWORD

by David J. Mason

These poems were written between November 1996 and September 1997. The majority of them were composed in sunnier climes during the Winter where the sunshine and equitable temperatures are ideal for nurturing the creative spirit.

It is not my intention to offend, merely to observe the foibles of our human race, hoping that we can build a fairer, more equal and humble society.

I dedicate "Waste" and "In the end" to you Mum, hoping you are proud of the work.

Best Wishes, 29/4/99.

GET A LIFE

GET A LIFE

I left with a piece of paper,
Owing six or seven grand.
I left with a First in Marketing,
They had my future planned.
In college I used to ask questions -
Who are we and why are we here?
And now that I know I will tell you,
There's really no doubting- it's clear
We're here to be responsible,
To earn a proper wage.
We're here to dwell in trivia
Until our dying days.
We're here to play the Stock Market,
To help us feather our nest -
And wear our badge, "Normality"
Like a fluffy cotton vest.
If we're lucky we rise to management
But all can play a role.
As a human race together,
Security is our goal.
So here I am, about to start,
What advice have I?
"Ask no questions, get stuck in
And watch it pile high!"

ENLIGHTENMENT

When small I would bawl and let it all out,
No knowledge of etiquette or embarrassment.
In my teens I would learn to keep it all in,
Practice suppression of my expression.
In my twenties and thirties society's virtue
Its dubious moral code
And then when I'm old
I can let myself go,
Do what I want to do.

But I write to tell you that's not how it is,
I saw my society falling to bits -
Corrupt with greed which comes straight from the top,
I jumped off the bus at the thirty-fifth stop.

ODE TO GEOFFREY BOYCOTT

For better that a man should
Keep his head down, looking for the 1s and 2s,
Than attempt to use his feet,
But with poor technique,
And do something daft
Like throw his wicket away.
Life is line and length.
Life is occupying the crease.
Slowly, slowly build a century.

BUY NOW, PAY LATER

Dull, dull and getting duller,
Someone show me the light.
Oh alright.

We have carpets and curtains
And wallpaper hanging
And painting and making
Some bright new ideas.
There are light shades
All coloured in new shades
And real glow fires
Sporting hot colours.

Blank, blank and feeling nothing,
Someone give me some soul.
Let the good times roll.

And buy, buy, buy while stocks last,
Snap up the crap whilst you can.
Fill all the empty space in your life,
Bury yourself in an eerie calm
Sever the nerves in your head,
Lose all feeling from neck to toe
Drown yourself in our water bed.

Dull, dull and getting duller,
Someone show me the light.
No, it's night.

A STRUGGLE

Do your best - that's all we ask -
There's always a demand for more.
From the cradle to the grave
We are subject to examination,
Entered for the wrong race,
An egg but no spoon.

Standing at the starting blocks
You wonder who's behind your promotion.
What is the logo you are carrying
And for whom? You were happy
Belonging to yourself, before elitism
Plucked you from a lower division.

How great are the rewards.
What years of practice it takes.
So in maturity the childhood promise dawns,
Contentment shuns the world's stage
And has little to do
With running a race.

THE REVOLUTION BEGINS

You didn't know,
You couldn't tell.
You thought my eyes were empty
And my ears stuffed solid
But I was quite permeable
In every pore, dissolving
Through every sense, absorbing,
Letting in more and more.
And because I did not answer,
You thought I was dumb.
And when I would not rage,
You took me for indifferent.
You had your torch,
I had seen my light
You wanted to save me from darkness,
I gave you a shining example.
Your principles rained down upon me,
Your dogma snapped at my heels.
Still I would not succumb,
Still I clung to the shadows
Of my own belief.
Never making clear,
Never forthright enough to tell
You were lost, fumbling in the dark.
Mine was not the street corner socialism,
The mouthpiece of petty politics.
Nor the dizzy heights of soapbox,
Only to be kicked to the ground.
Rather be silent, be still.
Use your ears and your eyes,
Maybe a motion or two,
Some calculated cajoling.
Don't give the game away.
I'm ready, I'm on my guard,
When the revolution comes, I am it.

SUICIDE

I thought of crying a pool of tears,
But I knew you wouldn't look.
Or you'd swear they were the crocodile type,
Though you'd never check for salt.
When the cloud bubbled about me,
You thought the future bright.
When I was crawling in the dark,
You'd say that life was light.
You saw my life through your eyes
And the images were fine.
When you find me swinging from this beam
You'll see my life through mine.

WASTE

I am biodegradable
And therefore able
To turn to dust
When my time is up.
I am organic;
Lay me down on your supermarket shelves,
I have never once eaten
Fertiliser.
I am part skeleton
And I have secret bones
Which only my maker
Knows.
I am a treasure;
Remember that
So that when I die
I can leave you all the bits I wasn't worth.
I am biodegradable;
Wash separately,
Always read the label.

IN THE END

You're halfway there
But don't know where you belong
And you're crying for someone or
Something you are missing
And then wonder what you are
Doing here in a restricted zone
Of uncertain individuals
Trapped in certain shells.
From time to time
A face or phrase knocks on your mind
And you are reminded
Of a life long gone
A plane away from the age to come.
But I'm busy investing in the latter
The souls of minions on future's platter
Serving time in another world
Even as I appear in this one.

GUTTER

Crawl crawl
In the gutter of life
And in the fag butt
Find a whole host of
What is the guts of life
And not the namby
Something they say it is
In the gardens of Eden.
Down in the dust
You can walk tall
Whereas with the whiter than white
You might just smudge the line
And lose yourself
On the printed page.

IN SUMMARY

Feel these fingers
And grasp the meaning
Of life there's nothing more
Than the nervous strings
Which lead you a dance
Through your puppet life.

UNIVERSITY CHALLENGE

Your starter for ten
And I'm boggered if I know
'Cause I wasn't there listening to Roman poetry
And I don't have an atlas in my head
Or dream of quotes Greeks once said.
When my only thought is of tea on the table
Or forty years of wasted work
Before my batteries ran dry.
You leave me speechless with your questions
But I have my hand on the buzzer
And reaching for the remote
I'll have the final say.

WORTH IT

A bob or two
An uncertain stake
On a horse
Who might just break a leg
Or fall at the first.
But let go the reins
And you'll see the rest of the field
Stopped still at the starting gate,
Admiring one another's hooves,
Picking stones from one another's toes.
Leap high to see a little more,
Don't laze grazing on the grassy fields
Where you finish up sticking to yourself,
Glued to the floor
Of the knacker's yard.

OUR MAN IN MAJORCA...

MY BUNION

You should stare at my Belisha bunion,
Red as a swollen beetroot,
Gnarled and knobbly and full of pain
And hanging around on my foot.

On of these days, I'll mash it up
And fill someone else's socks
So that they can feel the same
Walking in my shoes,
Or rather sandals
Because bunions won't wear it.

You should tread the path of life
With the bunion, mile after mile.
Bony and blistered and cut to bits
With his ugly, sardonic smile.

DEATH VALLEY

Because it was quite hot,
Because of the steep descent
And the same route in reverse
You thought of thirst
And the water we didn't have.
I pointed out we were far from dehydration
And only three kilometres from the supermarket.
Still you maintained you were dying
For a drink
But I knew we'd live, we were a thousand miles
From Death Valley.

A LESSON

A school of swimmers
Left from the shore,
They nodded and waved
And swam out some more,
But this school of swimmers
Learnt nothing, instead
They hid from their teacher
Upon the sea bed.

POOLS

Pools of rock,
Pools of tears
Of salt water,
Swimming pools
For fresh bathing
In tidal pools.
Pooled resources
Or motor cars pooled
In Liverpool.
You win some,
You pool some.

BIG RED BOOTS

I bought them in San Sebastian
Where Columbus set out for his goal.
He was off to see the New World,
I was planning an afternoon stroll.

He found out quite a bit over there
But I discovered more.
With the air-cushioned system inside my sole,
I could float above the floor.

He came back to Spain a hero,
At last he had the proof.
When I flew back to England in big red boots,
They said, "What a strange-looking goof!"

THE RED FLAG

We'll keep the red flag flying
And you'll keep swimming,
Deaf to the drum roll of pounding waves,
Blind to the bruising of jagged rock.
In the tug of war you are losing ground,
On shore we are secretly concerned.
Current opinion has it you are unaware
Of your fading fast from view.
Fish have fins and gills,
Your clumsy body wouldn't last long underwater.
So I'm calling for a helicopter, and comrade
We'll keep the red flag flying here.

RED WINE

It's the unravelling of mind
Which takes the time.
That's why we have red wine
To help us unwind.
A cut above Double Diamond.
It's alive!
It must be allowed to breathe
But once opened, it soon expires,
So quickly I connect the wires
And compose in the knowledge
That two brains are better than one.

JUST LIKE WORDSWORTH

Wordsworth, late of Windermere, poet.
Like the lunes of Lancaster,
Secret scribes working south of the Lakes
Coming to rest under the M6
Where their words of wisdom
Fill the concrete hoarding.
I make pilgrimage to this tunnel
And in it read the history,
A spattering of nausient spray paint,
Telling a story of constant change.
And I read the latest news
Learning that nothing stays the same
In this land of lost poets
Whom I've never chanced to meet,
As much a mystery as Wordsworth himself.

ALL THINGS BRIGHT
AND BEAUTIFUL

"December Skyline"

THE TREE THAT HOLDS UP THE SKY

How tired he is;
Black and bruised,
Arthritic and bowed
Down by gravity.
The weight of it all
Bending back
The creeping fingers
Stubbed short
By Winter's freezing wind.

Each Summer
He stretches out.
Welcoming green digits,
Fresh from Spring green mitts,
And he flourishes,
Tearing away the clouds,
Revealing a warm blue
Of high hopes.

By Autumn he is worn,
The fingers lose their fading flesh -
Poisoned from within,
Withering, brown and yellow skin.

He cowers from the bolt
Of lightning.
He winces at
The woodpecker's beak.
Billions burrow in his bark.
Hurricanes rip his limbs.

He stands firm,
He does not crack.
God gives him strength
To hold the heavens aloft.

DECEMBER SKYLINE

Someone drew a line in the sky,
Stratus grey above
Clear blue below,
The divide running from church tower to tree top.
Two territories, one dark
One light.
A marauding mist moves and in a moment
Dense droplets smudge,
Smear a wet finish,
Washing the heavens into one.

WINTER'S WORDS

Winter is walking toward you,
Stalking, the form of a black shadow
Threatening, the daylight shortening
Quick, take a torch or a candle,
Look for a hole in the night.
But carbon colours the canvas,
Settles solid in every pore
Till the grey wash of a weak dawn.
Then the heavy lids of a smoke-eyed sky
Drizzle tears soaking sodden landscapes
Of cold leaching from every cell.
So Winter sits upon you,
Drains away traces
Of light and warmth and love of life.
But though Winter bombards,
The sting is not that of X-rays
And a tiny kernel of optimism
Awaits a Spring outing.

ORANGE

Nothing but orange
In the last shreds
Of daylight,
Making a marmalade sky.
No blue, no white,
Just a dusky cone
To concentrate the eye
And seal the jar
Now that night is nigh.

AFTER THE RAIN

Night rain, rivulets ran and
Stones swam to a muddy bank in the middle.
Our feet feeling for the soft gaps,
Essential for a safe descent.
About us the woods are black
With the settled dust
And in the undergrowth
The moisture lingers in secret lairs.
Freshly fallen chestnuts sparkle as brown diamonds,
The spiked husks lie destitute and empty
Sure to be preyed upon by Nature,
Litter swallowed up by Mother Earth.
Then the smell of pine to ease the muscles,
Like the minerals from the bath tub
And eucalyptus penetrating,
Clearing the airways.
Finally as we emerge from the forest
There is the wafting olive smoke
To delight the dancing senses.

NEW YEAR'S DAY

I saw the sun rise on New Year's Day.
Fine flurries of cinder snow
Alighted, kissed and melted.
Finger tips with faint feeling frozen to nothing
And all the time waiting for warmth
Wasted on another hemisphere.
And here, here I stand alone against the ice,
A sole witness to another year of daybreak.
But my heart is lively, my liver warm inside me.
And when I think of something grey and cold
And lonely and sad and nearly dead,
I think of hangovers, pounding inside a thousand heads.

THE CONSERVATORY

From your glass capsule
I see billowing blossoms flaunting,
Fertility forecasting fruit aplenty
And clematis painting pink pantiles,
All to the rhythm of rain.
Such a setting for poetry
And for tea,
Followed by a finger of shortbread
Like soapy sandstone
Then you tell me of the bust you broke,
The skull snapped clean in two.
It was an accident
- But I can't believe you'd let such a thing happen here.
I take my books and walk away
Into the twilight.

CONSIDER THE LILIES OF THE FIELD

A floral tribute to my age
With legs like tap roots
Dancing in the swamp of Woodstock.
A posy with perfumed head,
A scent out of San Francisco
To stem the tide of hate and war
And a ribbon to make myself a present
To peace and love.
We are but the flowers of the field
Who come and go
So give us soft petals
And caring tendrils
To bind us together in love.
Help us to photosynthesise in secret
Shunning our darker side
So that if the surgeon cuts us open
He won't find blood but xylem and phloem.
Stand straight in your vase,
Show us your colours.
Never again would we hear the song
"Where have all the flowers gone
"Long time passing"
But the hum of flower power
Flowing through God's fields.

AND A COLD WIND BLOWS

On this blow away day
Words are thrown away,
Swallowed whole in the throat
Of a sandpaper wind
Whistling with teeth unkind,
Biting through soft tissue,
Tapping to the bone
Through every open channel.
I turn my face,
Raise my collar,
Don my scarf
And hat and gloves
And run for cover,
But he is all over.
When I close my door
He is still there,
Breathing hard about
My letterbox.

PHEW!

It's raining, it's pouring
And the hot air is exploding
Mixing up humidity
Making me feel stickicky.
My legs feel heavy,
My head is tired and empty
And my furnace lungs are bellowing.
This summer cauldron needs quenching
With cats and dogs and buckets
And every ocean chucked at it.
So stand and deliver,
You mighty stratosphere,
For in dancing my rain dance
I have my Creator's ear.

THE BUDDLEIA

London, London far away
And when you finally arrive
Has nothing to say
You haven't heard before.
Moving in circles
With the brash and busy
These colourful people flowering
For a season.
There are bus-loads of them,
Londoners living on the edge
Jumping up and down
And coming to rest on tube tracks.
I tested them for signs of life
Only the deep groan of a whalebone terminus
And the waving of sentry buddleia
On the line from Liverpool Street.

ALL CREATURES GREAT AND SMALL

"A Real Buzz"

THREE HARES

Three hares ran,
Ear and leg
Long and strong
In beauty of being and motion
On a hot crust
Under a lemon sun.
I picked them off
With my polished weapon,
One by one.
Three men run
And two of them
Are chasing one
Who trips in terror
On the ruined rubble
And is struck dumb
By the double blast,
Each one a flash from a polished gun.

SKYLARK

Skylark rides the rollercoaster
From Heaven's twin towers
To surface upon the Earth.
He sings a picture book scene,
Dangles from the finest of threads,
Dreams in shades of green,
Bids us take our rest.

DOG IN A FOURTRAK

Dog in a Fourtrak
Riding real high,
Master at the wheel
Says you are what you drive.

There's one for the master
And one for his dame
And tons of shining steel
Parked on commuter lane.

"Woof off" says the dog
Beep, beep on the horn,
We'll pin you to our bull bars
As we take the world by storm.

THE LOCUST WITH ONE LEG

Smiled, naturally
At a photo opportunity
Then carried on staring ahead
Like a locust who was dead.
But I was pleased to see
He later winked at me
And I carried him out on a towel
Thinking, how foul
Being one-legged is looked on as quirky
But to leave without washing is nothing but dirty.

THE WALKERS

He wore a flat cap and mac
With a high collar in Winter
And in Summer
He kept his jumper.
I watched from my window,
From the shadows of my life
Where early retirement was a euphemism
For enforced indolence and endless dreaming.
His routine kept me awake,
Split sections through the day
So that I knew when to eat
And when to read,
When light would shine
And darkness fall.

Still the dog padded through every season,
Faithful, never faltering year after year.
His master's voice I never heard,
He would woof for the two of them.
He was the man's best friend,
For in receiving the admiration of other folk
He became a social lifeline
And his master followed his lead.

Then suddenly I saw him no more.
Lost without his pet, I discovered dead.
Leaving me alone.
It was then I decided I must have
A dog of my own.

SEGREGATION

To me life is black or white,
I have no grey matter,
I see the cat, sat
Upon me, black and white,
One or the other.
And when I dream
It is in monochrome
With nothing in between.
So please, Martin Luther King -

Don't try to colour my opinion.

IN THE BAY

I do, I like simple things,
Like thirty minutes spent
Looking into the stalk eyes
Of crabs, survivors crawled ashore,
But Heaven knows what for.
What were they doing there
When the sea was full of air
And wet and warm with micro-fare?
They waved their pincers
And danced for us,
Never expecting reward or
Cheers, or swearing of oath
Never to eat crab sandwiches
Served on Cromer's sunny shores.
They didn't swim for us though,
I expect they were too tired.

OBSERVATION UPON, AND ADVICE TO, ONE OF LIFE'S SURVIVORS

What is it wasp?
You flying freak.
December is upon us,
It's time to take a break.
Go bunker up,
Hide underground,
It's nothing above freezing,
Too cold to make that sound
Of busy buzzing
In empty air.
The harvest gone,
The snow is here:

To warmer climes,
Head South young man
Be bold, be brave, don't tarry
And die here like an also-ran.

A REAL BUZZ

We called on Keith, a gang of us,
White hunters with jam jars
Treading trails behind half-formed houses
Where Nature hid from the digger.

It was sunny after tea, still flying
Looking for their own food,
Tables set in flower heads where
Pollen stained their tablecloths.

We tried not to scrunch them,
Tried not to get stung by them.
They flew from nectar drunk with delight
Into jam jars with the lid shut tight.

We clasped our treasure
Trying to add to the number
Of stripes and stings,
Of majestic moths and insect things.

Listen to the buzz of the little creatures,
The enigmatic sound
Of a hundred insect hearts a-beating
Before the digger bites the ground.

OLD EGGHEAD

Old egghead
Tramps on our street
Talks to himself
In his shell
That's how you can tell
He's not all there
So much so that he scares
Our careful shoppers.
You could smash his brains in
And he wouldn't feel it
And he doesn't talk any sense
Only mutters about the time it is in Moscow.
I saw him smiling
And wondered what he had to be happy about.
He stopped to show me his wristwatch
"Made in China
By a prisoner
Bad, bad Beijing".

THE ENEMY WITHIN

The dumb dog barks,
Like some deep-throated smoker,
Throwing curses to the wind.
Answers with an echo
To the empty space in his head.
The dumb dog replies,
Replays through the hollow air
And hears his shriek again.
Once more he hurls the vocal cords,
Affronted by the audacity
Of an enemy,
A stranger lurking out there.

The idiot yells,
And like the dumb dog,
Reflects his own paranoia.

DECORUM

"Middle-Aged Women are the Rudest"

TRYING IT ON

In this sacred semi-light
She slithers from one set to another.
Moving in and out of her wardrobe,
She is a clothed chameleon.
Any degree of discomfort will do,
"But do make me beautiful", she whispers
And tries to tie tight or hang loose,
A warm-blooded manikin.
The mirror though is silent
Reflecting indecision, posing questions,
Taking away the edge,
Leaving a nebulous notion.
Too smart, too formal, dressy.
Too rough, too ready, messy.
It makes me fat, it makes me thin.
It exposes, hides, the me within.
The hair's high up, the hair hangs down,
The natural look or the sultry clown.
The shoes stacked up, high heel or low,
In the world of fashion no yes or no.

The tide of time, one final look,
She sighs at all the size and shapes.
She is toying with a glimpse of perfection
Yet cruelly exposes her body's wants
For a flatter tummy
And a fuller bust,
Curving thighs
And a pert behind.

Lying naked in his arms,
Her flesh moulded with his,
She gazes at the discarded heap
And turning to face him
Smiles and wonders
How it ever could have mattered.

FASHION

What's that you're wearin'?
A smile
That ain't cool,
Wipe it away.

What's that you're takin'?
Huh? Food.
You make me sick,
Don't eat it.

What's that you're havin'?
A baby.
Well honey, hold that pose
For the camera.

A GOOD PARTY

You cram into the kitchen,
Dance in the dining room,
Tip-toe through the toilet.
Harassed in the hallway,
Collect again in the kitchen,
Puke in the passage way.
Collapse upon the couch,
Sleep upon the stairway,
Wake up with the winos.
Die out in the darkness,
Wish you were at home,
Tucked up and all alone.

HOLIDAY HOPES

Hims and hers
String ties in the swimming pool
And pass love's plastic globe
Feigning fear at the skimming splash
And girlies scream for men
To save their soluble make-up
And in doing so brush
The scales of their mermaid
Who wags her tail and waits
With Martini eyes and a kiss at the bar.

MIDDLE-AGED WOMEN ARE THE RUDEST

I'm in the dinner queue.
Well how do you do?
"All the worse for seeing you,
Here have an octopus arm and an elbow too."

Speechless, all I can think is "who, who..."
"Who are we? We are two two
Middle-aged ladies who ooh, ooh
Make upper class noises,
Moo, moo, moo".

EITHER WAY, IT STINKS

His armpits had the class of odour
Shared by my cooped-up Skoda.
All that engine waste, the oil and the gas
Slowly diffusing from the stinking mass.
He ambles, circumventing the table,
My sideways crab-scuttle declares I'm unable
To loiter at length within his zone
And to share his pungent pheromone.
Real men deal in dirt,
Have acrid armpits made to flirt.
Or perhaps they use those smelly sprays
Like the Feu Orange for Skoda ash-trays.

OUT DAMN SPOT

I take you spot where e'er I go,
You'd stop me spot
From making friends with debutantes
And showing my sartorial spoils
Which you've soiled
By yellowing my laundered skin.,
Popping up as a pin prick,
Massaged by curious fingers,
Weeping wet nothing on squeezing
Hard between index and thumb.
Fooled am I, foiled again.
You will not deliver of your sickly contents
So I wait, take a nap.
Pounce upon your unsuspecting form,
Press the pus from out of you,
Harder and harder and longer,
Choking the very life out of you.
And now you're a ruddy mess.
I'd plaster you up
But that would only draw attention to you.
Instead I will expose you to all my friends
And introduce you as
My fashionable bacterial friend
"Staphylococcus"
Whose unpronounceable name translates as
"The yellow one".

And having a yellow one
Is fun
And then they'll all be queueing
To have their face done.

THE GIFTED CHILD

Hush, child hush.
Stop spilling those dirty words,
Snaring on our drumming ears.
For when God gave gifts
He gave you the gab
And I am more than pleased
To cut you short with a clap
Of my hand
On your head,
One more sound and you're dead.
So put away your present
And hold your tongue
Whilst your mother and I
Discuss your future.

SCENE FROM A POSH PARTY

"How do you do?"
"It's something innate,
A will to carry on
No matter what,
Through thick and thin,
Rain or shine,
Famine or feast,
Good times and bad."

"What do you do?"
"I inhale and exhale.
I walk and I talk.
I eat and I drink,
Sleep and think.
And then I excrete,
It makes life complete."

"Yes, yes but what do you do,
What's your profession?"

"Avoiding the day of my life's cessation".

STOP, LOOK AND LISTEN

Hey, hey what's that with those lazy bones,
Lazing 'bout in this sunshine
With the wires snaking your chest, the earphones
Plugged up and nodding off.
And feet tapping to a special time,
One that I can't hear and wouldn't want to,
Something that stops you from serious pursuit,
Some rock'n'roll,
A singer on drugs and your life on the dole.

Wait a minute, hush now, listen.
It's not the vocals, guitar, keyboards or drum beat,
It's the whole, the thing which sends
You walking on the sidewalk of another street
Which is paved with gold,
The sort of stuff you could never meet
Sticking closer to home
And loafing the same old road.
Let me put it another way:
It's another world, a world of art,
And it's your congenital deafness
Which makes you a boring old fart.

THE CONCERNS OF A FRONTBENCHER

If they displayed my thoughts on a video screen
I'm afraid I'd be in trouble.
There'd be naked forms in erotic poses
Lodged inside my thinking bubble.

If they hooked me up and showed the truth
And the picture appeared quite frank,
When there weren't the forms in erotic poses
The screen would show a blank.

Here I sit whilst you shuffle your papers
And it's only just begun.
Oh please PM, no questions this time,
I just want to go out and have fun.

HUMILITY

I don't want to watch blockbuster movies.
I don't want to know about Hollywood star signs
Or supermodels' secrets,
Fringe meetings for fat politicians,
All of them trying to make more of a name for themselves.
I am not bowled over by French fashion designers
Or the prospect of gala dinners
And a chance to meet Oscar winners,
Or to listen to the admissions of alcoholic footballers
Dribbling at their spiralling wage bill.
I do not adhere to dress code
But instead prefer the naked truth:
Earls and their like should earn their money,
All silver spoons removed from mouths at birth,
Replaced with humble plastic.

APPEARANCES CAN BE DECEPTIVE

Cooking in the kitchen,
Moulding meals from ingredients
Caught napping in warm recesses,
Then slapping them on a plate
Where they sit and wait
For saliva to flow
And jaws and jowls
To grind out a taste
Of something fitting a description
Of the thing you are about to eat,
Or not as the case may be.

The waitress returns with a chicken curry.
"She'll not have it, she says it's not hers"
"Is that my fault?"
"She says so"
Says I'd better have another go,
It wasn't chicken, it was vegetable tacos.

"Madame, the chef will hear no more of it.
This expert labour of love, this dexterity
Fashions mystery beyond understanding.
Now believe and eat
And no more of this.
It is you who cannot see straight,
Believe in the tacos upon your plate".

Later:
"Now how was the meal, how do you feel?"
"Quite, quite strange as though some change
Crept over me and I could so easily
Have tasted chicken curry
In the tacos on the plate before me".

REAL MEN TAKE SPEED

Don't look now
Behind you!
But where?
Filling the frame of the rear-view mirror,
Isn't he ugly
In a snarly way.
Nose squashed on screen
Mouthing insults, hey
Hey, in my way,
Move your ass
Out of my road
Let me pass.
I smell testosterone,
I see big all-male
And his car is big boots
And he's going to crush me, the snail.
I'm moving over
Can't bear that face
Or the practised hand signals
As he lets out his gas.

Be careful now!
Ahead of you.
Take a look,
Across the road.
The BMW mangled,
I'm not sure about the load.

ANOTHER DAY AT THE OFFICE

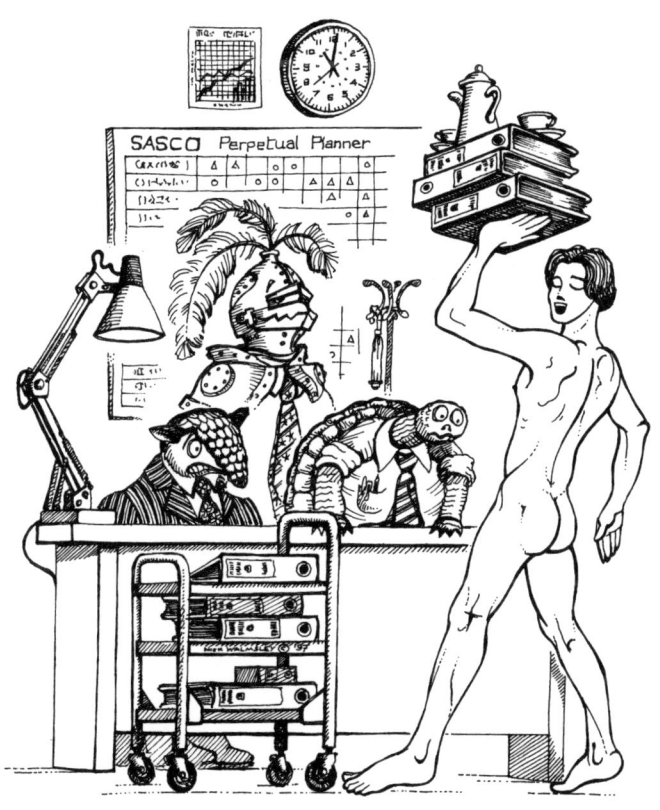

"Power Dressing"

A CORPORATE KISS

A peck on the cheek
Fell smack full on my lips
And what I proffered out of duty
You felt your duty to abuse.
To swallow me flesh and blood
Leaving a shadow skeleton
To carry to retirement's grave.
But I won't let you use your tongue
I can smell your breath a mile away.

POWER DRESSING

Inside the suit of armour
And the sheen of your shirt
Is a helpless skin.
But will you save it
By secreting yourself
In your Armani shell,
Or risk shame
By undressing in the office?
We could all share
In a naked defence
And letting loose this sham,
We could cease to be staff
And instead order ourselves
As if we had no clothes to put on.

MISSION STATEMENT

Part 1

It came in a cargo from the U.S. of A.
And on it they marked:
Top Secret; Urgent; Do not delay;
The latest export from the land of our dreams
Would save this nation,
Stop it falling apart at the seams.
The problem was guidance, we needed it bad,
We were so subjective,
It made our successful cousins sad.
Now they had written two words, the new Messiah
To deliver our souls, set our hearts on fire.

Part 2

A mission statement is what you need,
If you haven't got one, you haven't lived.
It's specific, it's measurable, objective enough,
It's not wishy-washy but hard-hitting stuff.

Man, now what's young junior doing here?
He's fuzzy, deluded, his life isn't clear.
Now help him write his statement today
Or just like a sinner, he'll fall by the way.

Part 3

I once had a mission statement,
It took three days to write,
And the day we lost that statement,
I swear I saw the light.

YOU WON'T WANT TO TALK TO ME

You, the apparition in my office,
On the look out for bonus points.
Head and body of a weasel,
One step nearer your prey
And pray, what is it you want?
Something pressing, of paramount importance?
But all I see and hear is you
Coming at me like a glove puppet.
Between the lines I read
Of your ability, stickability,
Suitability, compatibility
And all set to the rhythm
Of my tired fingers
Drumming, drumming on the desk.
I dream of your going,
I wish you away
But your mouth is still moving,
Advertising your wares.
Effluent oozes from your silver tongue,
Washing your words onto me,
Tired of your patronage and others
Who stick with suckers to their masters.
Whether I am good or bad,
Whether you respect me or not,
What does it matter?
So long as I can put you about.
So clear off and don't come back,
I don't want to know when you've made it
And when in the course of events
You have sold your soul to all and sundry,
Don't come sneaking around here
Asking to borrow mine.

COMPANY MAN

Bury me under a tonne of your paper
Save all I said on a Dictaphone
Put me on file and look at me later
Tell me the job that I'm doing's well done.
Send me a fax of a feeling or two
Wish me a get well and hope it is soon
Picture me sending it back to you
A crazy reply from your man in the moon.
Raise me up with the challenge to come
Alter my ego with company name.
The present's unwrapped and my life is undone
I hate to think of you taking the blame
For the job that's been done
Which has broken my heart
And the cost? There is none,
Once you stop you can't start.

.

THE QUESTIONNAIRE

They wanted some feedback
So I gave it to them.
Hardhitting, all the way to the boundary,
Crossed the rope.
Comments from a spectator's view,
Not a team player
Going through the motions.
These were emotions -
Angry word pictures on paper,
Free from the taint of peer pressure.

They guaranteed anonymity, no recriminations,
But soon after I was substituted.
The invisible hand of fate helped me
Through reception's revolving doors.

PLAYING FTSE
UNDER THE TABLE

"How to Bake an Imoral Cake"

FILL IN THE GAPS

Something has gone wrong -
There's a space
Full of succulent cacti, scrub sinewy green -
Which has not been built upon.
It's our decision without planning permission
To implement our vision
Which has always been short-sighted
And left the land a trifle blighted.
There's no need for tower block building,
No-one would want to live here
But with marketing hype and some keen competition,
We will not be outdone by our peer.

Oh give us a fishing village quaint!
With reinforced concrete , breeze block, fresh paint,
We'll turn it into a tourist city,
Where the gaps are filled in but the flowers are pretty.

PAPER RICHES

Economic growth,
That's what we like best.
Imaginary wealth,
An expanding treasure chest.
Don't let the pot boil over,
Simmer slowly on low flame.
Collect and store and buy some more,
You're a winner in life's game.
Go ahead with your investments,
Go ahead and make your day.
Making money is all consuming,
Eat it up if it gets in your way.

Say I heard it on the grapevine,
Say there's gonna be a crash.
What's that you're telling me mister?
I can't buy nothing with the cash.

HOW TO BAKE AN IMMORAL CAKE

Get the people of a nation to collect a wide variety
Of expensive ingredients.
Persuade the people the ingredients aren't really theirs.
Grease the palms of the people with a dubious
Promise of a considerable share of the cake.
Place cake on Stock Market.
Leave cake until risen in value ten times over.
Then hold up cake as an example of nation's successful baking.
Sack the majority of cooks, throw crumbs to the rest.
Finally cream off the icing and place in Government coffers.

This cake makes a lovely treat for shareholders,
Helping them to get fatter than ever.
It also makes an immoral nation greedy
For a slice of the same.
This Government does bake exceedingly immoral cake.

WEAPONS OF WAR

Are big money,
Good news for the unemployed,
Crafted elements of new technology,
Deterrents in experienced hands.

The men of war
Are tragically maimed.
Shot down or cut to bits,
Losing limbs,
Look - no hands!

Weapons of war are always wanted
And always given
By Western countries just like ours.
The Devil's making, an evil art
From the men who sell murder and haven't a heart.

MUNICIPAL SPORTS CENTRES THEY FAILED TO BUILD

Oh yes they could use it
But would it make a profit?
Would it pay? We ask,
Is it worth the risk?
Is there short term gain?
We can ignore the long term pain.
Then again we could shelve it
And wait for the moment
When private investment
Will make us this present,
With strings attached.

There's play as you pay
At an ever increasing, increasing rate.
Or a membership entitlement
For the physical enlightenment
Of the monetary fit
And not for the masses who learn bit by bit,
In this human race they've been left behind
And freedom of choice is all in the mind.

THE WORKING MAN AND WOMAN OF NO FIXED CLASS

So happy are we
To slave for you
At knock-down wages
You would laugh at.
But you're not joking
When you ask it of us
And tell us we're the lucky ones.
They're queueing to take our place
And we do believe it is our place
To labour for little reward.
For is it not decreed
There will always be the rich
And we will always have the poor
And you are what you are born
And through birthright you have become
Our leaders, those who would think for us
And piss on us, the nation's dross.

IN THE PSYCHIATRIST'S CHAIR

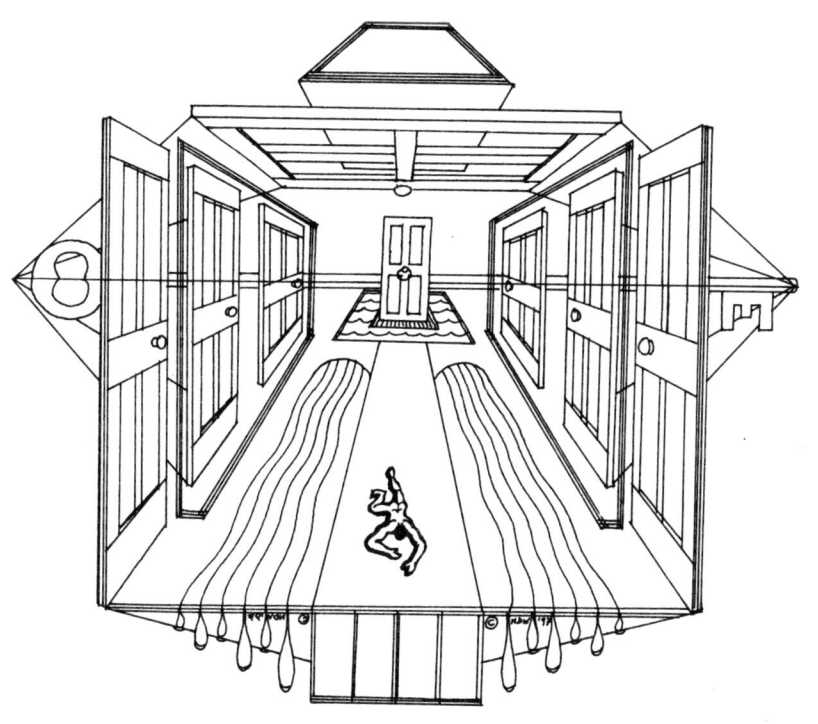

"Who Goes There?"

A DEN

Turn the corrugated tin
To the time-warped brick
And you have the same
Safe haven secure without.
Pitch up and disappear
For forty sublime winks
And wish you never wake
To face the mess they're making.
Sit up, curl back, tune in,
Sing the song of you heart
And find a familiar comfort
In the heat of your own sun.
Watch for invaders
Wait for sundown
And a certain safety
When you won't hear the crackling of branches
From the pressure of foreign feet,
Or the rattling upon your door
In the fist of a friendly neighbour or two.

A BREAK IN

Forced entry in the hallowed night.
The criminal rolls away the stone,
Climbs in, crawls through tiny tunnels
To find the nerve centre
Lit by the flickering
Of the mind's motion movies.

Uninvited, he crashes the camera lens,
Is part of the set.
Leading, he never suited
A supporting role, his sharp image
Larger than life, fills your screen
And you scream!

And wake
With a fluttering eye and a hammer heart.
He is gone,
I haven't seen him for years.
He may return,
For at night, whilst sleeping,
I sometimes leave the door wide open.

THE KNOWLEDGE

You were so radiant
On the day you were wed.
Joy beyond belief at the life
Of a child in your arms.
All your life you were
Happy with yourself,
And when I told you I was leaving
You smiled and said, "I know."

PUT THE PAST BEHIND YOU

I paid to see a psychologist friend,
He was fat, his hair was thin.
I told him my life was about to end,
He sighed and poured me a gin.
"Here's the tonic, let's share a glass,
I'm sure I know what you need.
You're suffering under the weight of your past,
A terrible load indeed.
Here take this," he gave me a jar,
Said, "Lock all those phantoms away.
The ghosts of your past are waging war,
You must learn to hold them at bay!
Take the jar to the highest peak,
Ceremoniously toss it below.
The stranglehold of the spirits break
And you are free to go."

I did as I was told to do
But the spirits leapt for life.
They survived my futile trap and so
Returned with double the strife.

Then I decided I'd try a new way,
Take the jar with me wherever I liked.
Open the top and let them have their say
Then shut up the spirits and close the lid tight.

WHO GOES THERE?

I can see through the windows
Without looking in.
Imagine myself crawling the corridors,
Creeping within.
Where once I wandered upright
And now a fugitive
Sent packing on the shivering river
Of lost love's tears.
Once all rooms held a view
From inside out.
Now in my mind a moat fills
About your door.
I am left in dreams alone
Turning the key,
Revealing a distorted plan,
A shadowy copy.
My spirit is hidden in your rooms,
Who knows where,
On which door the fist fights
To be heard.
Only time will deliver me
From sleepy visits,
And move my soul onwards
To a new home.

WILLIAM WON'T TELL

Her lips should be licking his,
Her mouth mixing with his.
Her eyes meeting with his,
His words tugging her heart,
Her mood made perfect by his words.
Her hopes rising with his breath,
Her fulfilment in his very being,
His body at one with hers.

William won't tell.
What is it William?
William I want you;
Where are you William?

Her lips lost in the shadows of black coffee,
Her mouth empty of explanation,
Her eyes vacant without expression.
Silence fills the seat,
Making her sink to her knees.
Sulking in the sorrowful air,
Her fast fading in his absence,
Her body in a black bag.

William won't tell.
What is it William?
William I need you.
When will you return?

WHO NEEDS DRUGS?

"The Message"

ATMOSPHERE

It's not the camera clicks
Or how far you've travelled
Or how much you know,
History and beauty,
Dramatic the scenery,
Perfect the company.

The warmth of it all
Can leave you cold,
A fruitless search
For a mysterious reward -
Just a feeling, a breath of atmosphere,
Caught upon a wind of change.

THE MESSAGE

In every language under the sun
Voluminous letters filled the sky
And the portent they carried, curt,
"The end of the world is nigh."
The neighbours came out to read the message,
They could only stand and sigh
And curse and swear at their ill-fated lives
And question as to why.
"Why oh why when we're having fun?"
Then I pronounced "It's just a lie!"
But inside I knew it was the truth,
I turned on the TV and waited to die.

THE DAY THE WORLD ENDED

The green and ordinary bus
Snakes between cement portals.
"Passengers take a last look
To your right, the sea,
A pall of mist and low flying cloud,
A wet grey mass, the end of the world."

As one we set function to flash.
The lens clicks, holds tight, the last light
Shut up.

FIRE AT THE LIDO

A blistering heat bubbled to boiling
Then slowly simmered.
Still the berry bodies bathed
In the sunshine shimmering.
First a cry split the air
Then a smoky cloud,
Followed by flames
And a hush hit the crowd.
They carried the torch
To the swimming pool,
The blackened body of
The tourist cool.
Help came too late,
There was nothing but steam;
And we heeded this warning,
One must wear sun cream.

THE BANANA-YELLOW ALLEGRO

Under deep blue skies we waited,
The sun singing a stately tune.
Necks are craned and breath is bated.
Who will be the first to catch
A glimpse of HM Queen Elizabeth
The Second

She arrives to a fluttering of flags and hearts
At the head of the motorcade.
The Royal Banana-Yellow Allegro -
She fits it like a glove
And steps out in glory
The first

To grace this stage, this monument
To rock'n'roll, the Bournemouth Hippodrome
Picking at the beat guitar
She plays a set like none before,
With Di at the mike
On backing

Vocals thumped out in revolutionary snarl,
Dylanesque she gives her all.
To massive applause
She throws her crown to the crowd
In encore proclaiming "And the first shall be
The last".

ADRENALIN

I am adrenalin,
Go Johnny go!
And you're twitchin', chatterin'
Don't you know
I have you by the short and curlies,
Won't let you slow,
Won't let you sleep
Go Johnny go!
With the flow.

I won't let you down
Follow my step on the floor
Dancing round and round
And go Johnny go!
Slow, slow,
Quick, quick, quick.

A NEW DAWN

"Exposure"

CARRY ON

This morning I am neutral, waving farewell
To the fickle fervour of yesterday.
But a routine finds its own rhythm
To disguise the want of any feeling
And sooner or later,
When no longer numb,
I'll have room for excitement,
The hard work's been done.

A CLEAN SWEEP

Winter vacations
I bring a brush,
A special sweep
And a nice soft duster
For clearing my thoughts
And raking rubbish from my subconscious.

During the night
I have to inspect the rubbish
Before it can be bagged
And sometimes the dusting
Makes me toss and turn
In my sleep.

The rubbish is left in black bags
Which the sandman collects.
All is spick and span
Ready to start the New Year.
The mess soon piles up again
But I can't afford a cleaner everyday.

DAYLIGHT

Day, when you're done
And you die, must you take the sun?
With him around it's a little lighter
And my outlook considerably brighter
When I can play out a lot longer
Instead of laying still at night
And darkness takes so long to turn to light.
He pretends to be friends
But I sense he would like to catch me off guard.
So I concentrate and stare ever so hard
Wait for the birdsong and the sun to show,
For when he comes a-knocking, you'll have to go.

EXPOSURE

One hot Summer and a seed is sown
Under the skin and between the ears.
A literary parasite lays eggs
And a plot is hatching
Of tiny creeping ideas,
Crawling like the ants in
The long grass where he lies.
Exposing himself to the heady concepts
Of blistering heat he can actually feel
In his lukewarm heart
One book, one afternoon
Primed with the knowledge
Of something more endearing .
More important than
All the things he had learnt
Wandering in the cold of his wilderness.

THE FIRST COFFEE

A dry dust of nothing
A light air of emptiness
My only thought confusion
Rain upon my palate
Bringing a stream of ideas
A flowing fullness
A new found philosophy.

FLASHBACK

From a song
And a mood
Comes a life
You still live
And you smile
To find yourself
Back
Where you began.

ON CLOSER INSPECTION

She saw sunshine in the brights of his eyes,
Thought of nothing underhand
In the cris-crossing of roving fingers
Exploring the shade beneath this table top.
His face floating like an angel's,
And his arms strong rope
To tie her in knots
And squeeze her like a love snake.
She couldn't see his cards,
Or the tricks he'd hidden up his sleeve,
But the lines upon his palms whispered
Of a shortfall somewhere in the future.

A LITTLE
GREEN PIECE

"Injuns' Revenge"

THE ELEVATED SECTION OF THE M4

Birdsong echoes in empty daylight.
Sunlight sings in sure reply.
Nature's radar fully functioning,
The groundswell of abundant life.
Mobilising, cats and dogs,
Unleashed they run for freedom
And babies and mothers and children
Are waking, walking, wide awake.
Everything living is breathing
In clean
And listening
To the new life.

The old has passed away,
The petrol-driven pulse
Ceased.
From now on only
The whirr of sleek bicycle wheels
Or the patter of feet
As the transport minister
Decrees
No more motors on roads like these.

WE NEED A BYPASS NOW! (PART 1)

The scrape of motor metal
On our minds.
The graze of gasoline
On our lungs.
The purr of piston
And brake drum beat.
The sticking jam
And crawler can.
Of humming steel.
Of cranking gears.
Of glazed windshields
Hiding dazed looks.

Radios rap in our sleep.
Diesel deliveries signal dawn.
Metal flows downstream.
We watch and wait
For high tide.

WE NEED A BYPASS NOW (PART 2)

The channel's unplugged.
Diverted, the contents flowed.
Only a stream trickled here
From time to time.
Then dam it!
A second blockage,
A vehicular embolism
Of heavy lorries loaded down,
Puffing and clogging,
Clogging and puffing.
And a growing leak
Is greeted by such angry signs
Set upon our holy lawns:
"We need a bypass
To bypass the bypass,
Now!"

KIDS WITHOUT LEGS

Kids without legs,
A thing of the past,
With decent food and medicine
The legs are sticking fast.
Adults without brains,
So it used to be,
The best education in Europe,
It's changing by degree by degree.
People without homes,
Absurd though this may sound,
The caring and sharing of Britain -
There's more than enough to go round.

Kids without legs,
It's come to pass,
Waving his joystick,
Never gets off his ass.
Adults who can't read or write,
I'm afraid we must confess.
Pay teachers less, provide them with less,
Leave them in a mess.
Streets are paved with homeless
As we celebrate our wealth.
While buildings lie empty and useless
We drink to our future, good health!

NO HOLES LEFT (IN THE BELT)

Picture this,
World demand in a tummy.
Now we all know that people buy things
Which are useless but taste rather yummy.
And tummy gets bigger
And bloats just a bit,
The countryside suffers,
Gets covered in shit.
And tummy keeps growing,
Better loosen his belt
But we all go on stuffing,
Ignoring the threat.
Until one day he's had enough.
Tough tummy starts talking,
Tough tummy gets tough.
He's waited and waited and waited enough,
It's the end of the world
As he vomits the stuff.

RECESSION IS A GOOD THING

You're earning less but
Your money's worth more
You're sharing your job
But you won't starve.
And when there's less in the kitty
You don't have to trouble yourself
To decide how to buy
Something you never needed.
And found hard to want.
The planet loves a lot of less,
Not the leftovers to swallow
And noxious waste from air:
The Earth wheezing through our excesses.
So here's to recession,
And a longer life for all.

INJUNS' REVENGE

Red Injuns a'comin,
'Cross the plains to Birmingham
They say there is no stopping them
Colonisin' our country ma'm.
They got tomahawks and bows and arrows,
They got murder in their eyes,
There's a thousand strong of them Indians
Went and took us by surprise.
Went and left their reservation,
Sailed on to Liverpool,
Said they'd teach us folks a lesson,
Said we were greedy, dumb and cruel.
See they've taken over parliament,
See their gonna rule our land,
Said revenge had waited a century,
Sure they had the whole thing planned.
But me, I kinda like it,
All them Injun decrees,
I moved out of dull old suburbia,

To one of them nice new teepees.

THINKING OF YOU

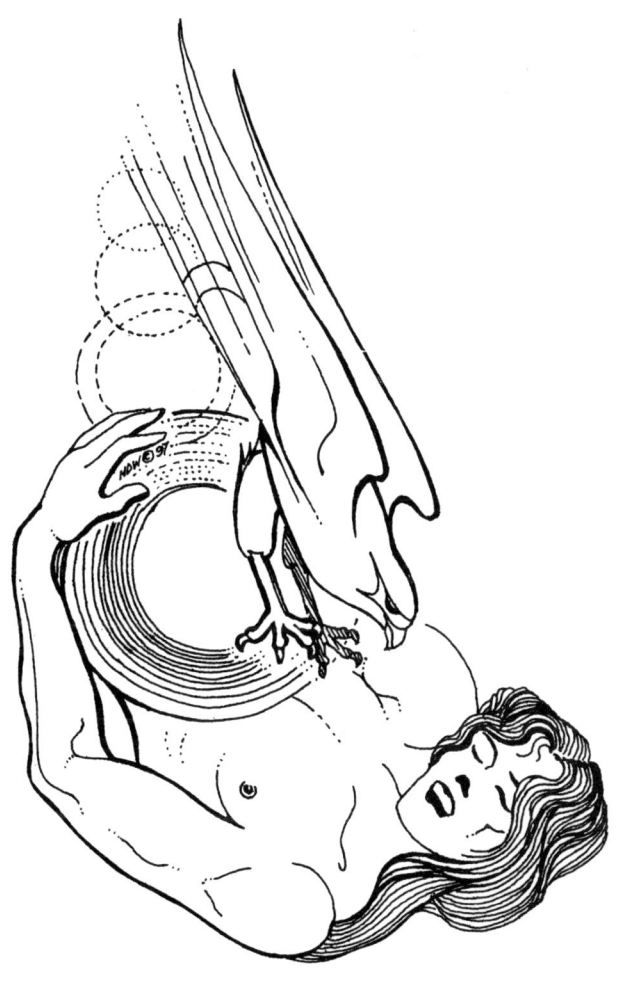

"For you, My Love"

THE PREACHER

Wears a beard
And paints weird
Crazy stuff on his canvas,
Then comes around and drinks tea with us.
Has visions abroad in exotic places,
The preacher I swear doesn't know what day it is.
His mind kinda fixed on a higher plane,
To dwell at our level, well that's just a pain.

OLD BLUE EYES

Old Blue Eyes is back
On a bar stool in Spain.
I walked right into him
And looked straight through him
Because I thought he was blind,
But then his eyes moved
Responding to the barman,
Ordering another one.
He looked at me,
I smiled politely
And he drank his whisky
Thinking, "That foreign geezer's staring at me."
Why oh mother, why
Did you give me this pair of reflective eyes?
I want to be alone,
Here in Pedro's café,
Fluttering eyes at pretty chicas
Instead of staring at my sneakers.

Poor old Pablo Blue Eyes,
I left him sitting on his stool.
Then I dived for the blue of his eyes once more
At the local swimming pool.

THE FIRST BEAT OF LOVE

Below deck I work
At your convoys
And I am a friendly sub
Swimming in your sea
Feeling my way
Through to the tiniest pulse
Under a clear membrane
Where your signal works
Out an unnamed rhythm
With a special tune
Which, if I'm correct
I am hearing loud and clear.

FOR YOU, MY LOVE

Oh! If he loved her
The wind would hold her,
A flying falcon or albatross
Rising on a thermal
Up there with the sun
And her pillow clouds.
She would wave to him below
And he would blow kisses,
Rising even as she,
Climbing to meet her.
And so she steels herself
And throws herself from her perch.
For a moment her heart beats
Fast as flapping wings
As she manages to hold her head aloft,
But her feet are falling,
She is leaping
Into his arms.

THE GIRL WITH THE CIGARETTE

Blows a smokescreen
And whistles a love tune
From the rose-tipped lips
At the funnel's edge.
You read her message
Loud and clear
It's not love she wants
Not on the bitten chapped lips
But a deep beer
To drown the sorrow of another
Lover lost for words.

LENZA PENNY (LEND ME A PENNY)

Tollo and Loffo back in seventy-three,
Extorting money from lads like me.
You could never relax in the playground see
For the fear of your hearing, "Lenza penny!"
"Lenza penny", "Er I 'aven't got any"
"Yer lyin' yer smart arse, we might get unfriendly."
"But I swear I spent it on dinner money",
"Come 'ead you lad, you're tryin' to be funny!"
"No honest, honest, I swear it's no lie!"
"Hey lad - you're gonna die!"
And with that Tollo put his eye to my eye
And Loffo, he strangled me with me own tie.
It was always the same, I paid up in the end
And Loffo and Tollo said I was their friend.
I never kept count of the ransom I paid them
But I know when I die my reward is in heaven.

LOVE MACHINE

She's hippy, she's pretty,
We're all set to dance.
I don't know your name love
But we're in with a chance.

We're rockin', we're rollin'
I hate all this stuff
But picking the chicks up
We all know it's tough.

Oh Heather, my angel
My lover and friend
You'd still go on dancing,
Thank God it's the end.

I'm blistered, I'm done in
But I've done my bit
Hey Heather you raver
Would you like to come sit

Down at my place
For a coffee or two.
"Sure, that would be lovely".
She fancies me too.

Say that's great then Heather,
It's not a long walk.
I could do with some fresh air
And a chance for a talk.

She looked at me worried and said,
"So no car". I said "no".
She said "See yer".
And I said "Ta-ra".

ONE TOO MANY

Every meniscus tells a story
And you're full up.
While I wait for you to start blowing bubbles,
You insist on a top-up.
But I know you and your little Vesuvius,
And as you erupt
I don't linger in the lava of Pompeii
But run like hell for the last bus home.

SOFTY

I'm a softy
Mould me
On your potter's wheel
And feel
Me like you
In all I think and do.

SOMEONE'S MOTHER

Someone's mother
Has eyes like black holes
And the RayBans she sports
Hide her suffering soul.
Vacant lady,
Hot hell at the wheel,
Pumping the gas,
Dulls the pain which she feels.
Lonesome lover,
Heart twisted with rage.
How much speed
This grief to assuage?
Tired loser,
Her spirit gives out.
The end of the road,
There is no need to shout.
Someone's mother
Met it with calm.
After racing through life,
She is glad of death's balm.

STRANGER

Never, never accept sweets
Or take a ride in a strange car.
Yet here we are,
You at the wheel, going nowhere
And me the awkward passenger
Chalk and cheese
On a night ride together.
Love's memories left in lay-bys
Passed me by.
Now I can only shiver in my seat
Hoping you deliver me safe and sound,
For I forgot my Mother's advice
When I said "Yes, I'd love to go out tonight".

A WASTED JOURNEY

I felt my way beneath starry skies,
Set my eyes against the blazing sun,
Carried myself aloft
Where others would have fallen.
I stumbled across the dry barranco,
Ran ragged amongst the teeming rocks,
Kept on and on
With no question of rest.
I lost two horses,
My third is lame.
I wore my way through two pairs of boots,
Straight through to the sole, so bad I had to shoot them,
Bandits took my third pair.
I am two inches shorter.
I drowned in the deepest, blue-est lake
But local fishermen landed me, hung me to dry.

Knocking at your door,
I see your mother's face
Pale and a shaking head
Bowing to the ground
"She does not want to see you,"
"Her eyes are shut tight,"
"She is perfectly still"
"As if she were dead."
"Oh I see," I said
And turned right around
To look for the nearest shoe shop.